One Happy Moment a Day

Ladybug Journals

One Happy Moment a Day is your journal for recording the happy things that occur in your life every day. They could be simple things like a phone call from a distant friend, an unexpected meeting with someone or some other little happy surprise. Record these happy moments in your journal, and soon you will look forward to each new day waiting for more lovely surprises.

We don't stop to notice the nice little everyday joyful moments that happen and we end up thinking life is boring and sad. Your happy memory journal will help you to zone in on the lovely events that you would otherwise miss. Train yourself to have a positive outlook on life with this happy memory journal. Record five years of happiness to reflect upon!

Date: _____

Example Page

There is a blank date at the top of the page, so you can start your five years of happy memories on any day that you want to.

~FIRST~
Fill in the month and day at the top of the page to get started.

~NEXT~
Fill in the current year, and write down anything that made you happy today in the daily entry. Then repeat these steps tomorrow on the next page.

20 __

_____
_____
_____
_____
_____

~AND~
When the year is over, simply start another year. Revisit your past happy moments while you record new ones.

20 __

_____
_____
_____
_____
_____

There are 365 pages for five years of happy memories and five daily entries on each page for each year.

As the next 5 years go by you can revisit your happy memories from the previous years while recording new ones.

Date _____

These Joyful Memories Belong To:

Name:

_____

Address:

_____

_____

Phone:

_____

Email:

_____

Date: _____

20 __ 🐞

_____
_____
_____
_____

20 __ ✿

_____
_____
_____
_____

20 __ 🐞

_____
_____
_____
_____

20 __ ✿

_____
_____
_____
_____

20 __ 🐞

_____
_____
_____
_____

20 __

_____
_____
_____
_____
_____

20 __

_____
_____
_____
_____
_____

20 __

_____
_____
_____
_____
_____

20 __

_____
_____
_____
_____
_____

20 __

_____
_____
_____
_____

Date: _____

20 __ 🐞

_____
_____
_____
_____

20 __ ✿

_____
_____
_____
_____

20 __ 🐞

_____
_____
_____
_____

20 __ ✿

_____
_____
_____
_____

20 __ 🐞

_____
_____
_____
_____

Date _____

20 __ 🐞

20 __ ✿

20 __ 🐞

20 __ ✿

20 __ 🐞

Date: _____

20 __ 🐞

_____
_____
_____
_____

20 __ ✳

_____
_____
_____
_____

20 __ 🐞

_____
_____
_____
_____

20 __ ✳

_____
_____
_____
_____

20 __ 🐞

_____
_____
_____
_____

Date _____

20 __ 🐞

---

20 __ ✿

---

20 __ 🐞

---

20 __ ✿

---

20 __ 🐞

Date: _____

20 __

20 __

20 __

20 __

20 __

Date _____

20 __

20 __

20 __

20 __

20 __

Date: _____

20 __ 🐞

20 __ ✿

20 __ 🐞

20 __ ✿

20 __ 🐞

Date _____

20 __ 🐞

20 __ ❀

20 __ 🐞

20 __ ❀

20 __ 🐞

Date: _____

20 __ 🐞

_____
_____
_____
_____

20 __ ✳

_____
_____
_____
_____

20 __ 🐞

_____
_____
_____
_____

20 __ ✳

_____
_____
_____
_____

20 __ 🐞

_____
_____
_____
_____

Date _____

20 __ 🐞

_____

_____

_____

_____

20 __ ❀

_____

_____

_____

_____

20 __ 🐞

_____

_____

_____

_____

20 __ ❀

_____

_____

_____

_____

20 __ 🐞

_____

_____

_____

_____

Date: _____

20 __

---

20 __

---

20 __

---

20 __

---

20 __

Date _____

20 __ 🐞

_____

_____

_____

20 __ ❀

_____

_____

_____

20 __ 🐞

_____

_____

_____

20 __ ❀

_____

_____

_____

20 __ 🐞

_____

_____

_____

Date: _____

20 __ 🐞

_____

_____

_____

20 __ ✿

_____

_____

_____

20 __ 🐞

_____

_____

_____

20 __ ✿

_____

_____

_____

20 __ 🐞

_____

_____

_____

Date _____

20 __ 🐞

_____
_____
_____
_____

20 __ ✾

_____
_____
_____
_____

20 __ 🐞

_____
_____
_____
_____

20 __ ✾

_____
_____
_____
_____

20 __ 🐞

_____
_____
_____
_____

Date: _____

20 __ 🐞

_____

_____

_____

_____

20 __ ✿

_____

_____

_____

_____

20 __ 🐞

_____

_____

_____

_____

20 __ ✿

_____

_____

_____

_____

20 __ 🐞

_____

_____

_____

_____

Date _____

20 __ 🐞

_____
_____
_____
_____

20 __ ✺

_____
_____
_____
_____

20 __ 🐞

_____
_____
_____
_____

20 __ ✺

_____
_____
_____
_____

20 __ 🐞

_____
_____
_____
_____

Date: _____

20 __ 🐞

_____

_____

_____

20 __ ✿

_____

_____

_____

20 __ 🐞

_____

_____

_____

20 __ ✿

_____

_____

_____

20 __ 🐞

_____

_____

_____

Date _____

20 __ 🐞

_____
_____
_____
_____

20 __ ❀

_____
_____
_____
_____

20 __ 🐞

_____
_____
_____
_____

20 __ ❀

_____
_____
_____
_____

20 __ 🐞

_____
_____
_____
_____

Date: _____

20 __ 🐞

_____

_____

_____

20 __ ✻

_____

_____

_____

20 __ 🐞

_____

_____

_____

20 __ ✻

_____

_____

_____

20 __ 🐞

_____

_____

_____

Date _____

20 __ 🐞

20 __ ✿

20 __ 🐞

20 __ ✿

20 __ 🐞

Date: _____

20 __ 🐞

_____
_____
_____
_____

20 __ ✿

_____
_____
_____
_____

20 __ 🐞

_____
_____
_____
_____

20 __ ✿

_____
_____
_____
_____

20 __ 🐞

_____
_____
_____
_____

Date _____

20 __ 🐞

20 __ ✿

20 __ 🐞

20 __ ✿

20 __ 🐞

Date: _____

20 __ 🐞

_____

_____

_____

_____

20 __ ✿

_____

_____

_____

_____

20 __ 🐞

_____

_____

_____

_____

20 __ ✿

_____

_____

_____

_____

20 __ 🐞

_____

_____

_____

_____

Date _____

20 __ 🐞

20 __ 🌼

20 __ 🐞

20 __ 🌼

20 __ 🐞

Date: _____

20 __ 🐞

_____

_____

_____

20 __ ✳

_____

_____

_____

20 __ 🐞

_____

_____

_____

20 __ ✳

_____

_____

_____

20 __ 🐞

_____

_____

_____

20 __

20 __

20 __

20 __

20 __

Date: _____

20 ___ 🐞

20 ___ ✳️

20 ___ 🐞

20 ___ ✳️

20 ___ 🐞

Date _____

20 __ 🐞

20 __ ✳

20 __ 🐞

20 __ ✳

20 __ 🐞

Date: _____

20 __ 🐞

_____
_____
_____
_____

20 __ ✿

_____
_____
_____
_____

20 __ 🐞

_____
_____
_____
_____

20 __ ✿

_____
_____
_____
_____

20 __ 🐞

_____
_____
_____
_____

Date _____

20 __ 🐞

_____

_____

_____

_____

20 __ ❀

_____

_____

_____

_____

20 __ 🐞

_____

_____

_____

_____

20 __ ❀

_____

_____

_____

_____

20 __ 🐞

_____

_____

_____

_____

20 __

_____
_____
_____
_____

20 __

_____
_____
_____
_____

20 __

_____
_____
_____
_____

20 __

_____
_____
_____
_____

20 __

_____
_____
_____
_____

Date _____

20 __

20 __

20 __

20 __

20 __

Date: _____

20 __

---

20 __

---

20 __

---

20 __

---

20 __

Date _____

20 __ 🐞

20 __ 🌼

20 __ 🐞

20 __ 🌼

20 __ 🐞

20 __

---

20 __

---

20 __

---

20 __

---

20 __

Date _____

20 __

_____

_____

_____

_____

20 __

_____

_____

_____

_____

20 __

_____

_____

_____

_____

20 __

_____

_____

_____

_____

20 __

_____

_____

_____

_____

Date: _____

20 __

---

20 __

---

20 __

---

20 __

---

20 __

Date _____

20 __ 🐞

20 __ ✾

20 __ 🐞

20 __ ✾

20 __ 🐞

Date: _____

20 __ 🐞

_____

_____

_____

_____

20 __ ✿

_____

_____

_____

_____

20 __ 🐞

_____

_____

_____

_____

20 __ ✿

_____

_____

_____

_____

20 __ 🐞

_____

_____

_____

_____

Date _____

20 __ 🐞

_____
_____
_____
_____

20 __ ✾

_____
_____
_____
_____

20 __ 🐞

_____
_____
_____
_____

20 __ ✾

_____
_____
_____
_____

20 __ 🐞

_____
_____
_____
_____

Date: _____

20 __

---

20 __

---

20 __

---

20 __

---

20 __

Date _____

20 __ 🐞

_____
_____
_____
_____

20 __ ✿

_____
_____
_____
_____

20 __ 🐞

_____
_____
_____
_____

20 __ ✿

_____
_____
_____
_____

20 __ 🐞

_____
_____
_____
_____

Date: _____

20 __ 🐞

_____

_____

_____

_____

20 __ ✿

_____

_____

_____

_____

20 __ 🐞

_____

_____

_____

_____

20 __ ✿

_____

_____

_____

_____

20 __ 🐞

_____

_____

_____

_____

Date _____

20 __ 🐞

20 __ ✿

20 __ 🐞

20 __ ✿

20 __ 🐞

Date: _____

20 __ 🐞

---

20 __ ✿

---

20 __ 🐞

---

20 __ ✿

---

20 __ 🐞

Date _____

20 __

---

20 __

---

20 __

---

20 __

---

20 __

Date: _____

20 __ 🐞

_____

_____

_____

_____

20 __ ✳

_____

_____

_____

_____

20 __ 🐞

_____

_____

_____

_____

20 __ ✳

_____

_____

_____

_____

20 __ 🐞

_____

_____

_____

_____

Date _____

20 __

20 __

20 __

20 __

20 __

Date: _____

20 __

_____
_____
_____
_____

20 __

_____
_____
_____
_____

20 __

_____
_____
_____
_____

20 __

_____
_____
_____
_____

20 __

_____
_____
_____
_____

Date _____

20 __ 🐞

20 __ ❁

20 __ 🐞

20 __ ❁

20 __ 🐞

Date: _____

20 __ 🐞

_____
_____
_____
_____

20 __ ✽

_____
_____
_____
_____

20 __ 🐞

_____
_____
_____
_____

20 __ ✽

_____
_____
_____
_____

20 __ 🐞

_____
_____
_____
_____

Date _____

20 __

20 __

20 __

20 __

20 __

Date: _____

20 __

---

20 __

---

20 __

---

20 __

---

20 __

Date _____

20 __ 🐞

_____

_____

_____

_____

20 __ ❀

_____

_____

_____

_____

20 __ 🐞

_____

_____

_____

_____

20 __ ❀

_____

_____

_____

_____

20 __ 🐞

_____

_____

_____

_____

Date: _____

20 __ 🐞

20 __ ❀

20 __ 🐞

20 __ ❀

20 __ 🐞

Date _____

20 __ 🐞

_____
_____
_____
_____

20 __ ❀

_____
_____
_____
_____

20 __ 🐞

_____
_____
_____
_____

20 __ ❀

_____
_____
_____
_____

20 __ 🐞

_____
_____
_____
_____

Date: _____

20 __

---

20 __

---

20 __

---

20 __

---

20 __

---

20 __

20 __

20 __

20 __

20 __

Date: _____

20 __ 🐞

_____
_____
_____
_____

20 __ ✺

_____
_____
_____
_____

20 __ 🐞

_____
_____
_____
_____

20 __ ✺

_____
_____
_____
_____

20 __ 🐞

_____
_____
_____
_____

Date _____

20 __ 🐞

_____

_____

_____

_____

20 __ ✾

_____

_____

_____

_____

20 __ 🐞

_____

_____

_____

_____

20 __ ✾

_____

_____

_____

_____

20 __ 🐞

_____

_____

_____

_____

Date: _____

20 __ 🐞

20 __ ❋

20 __ 🐞

20 __ ❋

20 __ 🐞

Date _____

20 __ 🐞

_____
_____
_____
_____

20 __ ✾

_____
_____
_____
_____

20 __ 🐞

_____
_____
_____
_____

20 __ ✾

_____
_____
_____
_____

20 __ 🐞

_____
_____
_____
_____

Date: _____

20 __

_____
_____
_____
_____

20 __

_____
_____
_____
_____

20 __

_____
_____
_____
_____

20 __

_____
_____
_____
_____

20 __

_____
_____
_____
_____

Date _____

20 __ 🐞

_____

_____

_____

_____

20 __ ✾

_____

_____

_____

_____

20 __ 🐞

_____

_____

_____

_____

20 __ ✾

_____

_____

_____

_____

20 __ 🐞

_____

_____

_____

_____

Date: _____

20 __ 🐞

_____
_____
_____
_____
_____

20 __ ✿

_____
_____
_____
_____
_____

20 __ 🐞

_____
_____
_____
_____
_____

20 __ ✿

_____
_____
_____
_____
_____

20 __ 🐞

_____
_____
_____
_____
_____

Date _____

20 __ 🐞

_____
_____
_____
_____
_____

20 __ ❀

_____
_____
_____
_____
_____

20 __ 🐞

_____
_____
_____
_____
_____

20 __ ❀

_____
_____
_____
_____
_____

20 __ 🐞

_____
_____
_____
_____

Date: _____

20 __

---

20 __

---

20 __

---

20 __

---

20 __

Date _____

20 __ 🐞

_____

_____

_____

_____

20 __ ✿

_____

_____

_____

_____

20 __ 🐞

_____

_____

_____

_____

20 __ ✿

_____

_____

_____

_____

20 __ 🐞

_____

_____

_____

_____

Date: _____

20 __ 🐞

_____
_____
_____
_____

20 __ ❀

_____
_____
_____
_____

20 __ 🐞

_____
_____
_____
_____

20 __ ❀

_____
_____
_____
_____

20 __ 🐞

_____
_____
_____
_____

Date _____

20 __ 🐞

_____
_____
_____
_____

20 __ ❀

_____
_____
_____
_____

20 __ 🐞

_____
_____
_____
_____

20 __ ❀

_____
_____
_____
_____

20 __ 🐞

_____
_____
_____
_____

Date: _____

20 __

---

20 __

---

20 __

---

20 __

---

20 __

Date _____

20 __

---

20 __

---

20 __

---

20 __

---

20 __

Date: _____

20 __ 🐞

_____
_____
_____
_____

20 __ ✾

_____
_____
_____
_____

20 __ 🐞

_____
_____
_____
_____

20 __ ✾

_____
_____
_____
_____

20 __ 🐞

_____
_____
_____
_____

Date _____

20 __ 🐞

_____
_____
_____
_____

20 __ ❀

_____
_____
_____
_____

20 __ 🐞

_____
_____
_____
_____

20 __ ❀

_____
_____
_____
_____

20 __ 🐞

_____
_____
_____
_____

Date: _____

20 __ 🐞

---

20 __ ✻

---

20 __ 🐞

---

20 __ ✻

---

20 __ 🐞

Date _____

20 __ 🐞

_____
_____
_____
_____

20 __ ❀

_____
_____
_____
_____

20 __ 🐞

_____
_____
_____
_____

20 __ ❀

_____
_____
_____
_____

20 __ 🐞

_____
_____
_____
_____

Date: _____

20 __

_____
_____
_____
_____

20 __

_____
_____
_____
_____

20 __

_____
_____
_____
_____

20 __

_____
_____
_____
_____

20 __

_____
_____
_____
_____

Date _____

20 __

20 __

20 __

20 __

20 __

Date: _____

20 __ 🐞

_____
_____
_____
_____

20 __ ✿

_____
_____
_____
_____

20 __ 🐞

_____
_____
_____
_____

20 __ ✿

_____
_____
_____
_____

20 __ 🐞

_____
_____
_____
_____

20 __ 🐞

20 __ ✿

20 __ 🐞

20 __ ✿

20 __ 🐞

Date: _____

20 __ 🐞

20 __ 🌼

20 __ 🐞

20 __ 🌼

20 __ 🐞

Date _____

20 ___ 🐞

_____

_____

_____

_____

20 ___ ✾

_____

_____

_____

_____

20 ___ 🐞

_____

_____

_____

_____

20 ___ ✾

_____

_____

_____

_____

20 ___ 🐞

_____

_____

_____

_____

20 __ 🐞

_____
_____
_____
_____

20 __ ✿

_____
_____
_____
_____

20 __ 🐞

_____
_____
_____
_____

20 __ ✿

_____
_____
_____
_____

20 __ 🐞

_____
_____
_____
_____

Date _____

20 __ 🐞

_____
_____
_____
_____

20 __ ✿

_____
_____
_____
_____

20 __ 🐞

_____
_____
_____
_____

20 __ ✿

_____
_____
_____
_____

20 __ 🐞

_____
_____
_____
_____

Date: _____

20 __ 🐞

_____

_____

_____

_____

20 __ ✿

_____

_____

_____

_____

20 __ 🐞

_____

_____

_____

_____

20 __ ✿

_____

_____

_____

_____

20 __ 🐞

_____

_____

_____

_____

Date _____

20 __ 🐞

20 __ ❀

20 __ 🐞

20 __ ❀

20 __ 🐞

Date: _____

20 __ 🐞

_____
_____
_____
_____

20 __ ✺

_____
_____
_____
_____

20 __ 🐞

_____
_____
_____
_____

20 __ ✺

_____
_____
_____
_____

20 __ 🐞

_____
_____
_____
_____

Date _____

20 __ 🐞

20 __ ✿

20 __ 🐞

20 __ ✿

20 __ 🐞

Date: _____

20 __ 🐞

20 __ ✿

20 __ 🐞

20 __ ✿

20 __ 🐞

Date _____

20 __ 🐞

20 __ ✻

20 __ 🐞

20 __ ✻

20 __ 🐞

Date: _____

20 __ 🐞

20 __ ✿

20 __ 🐞

20 __ ✿

20 __ 🐞

Date _____

20 __ 🐞

_____
_____
_____
_____

20 __ ✿

_____
_____
_____
_____

20 __ 🐞

_____
_____
_____
_____

20 __ ✿

_____
_____
_____
_____

20 __ 🐞

_____
_____
_____
_____

Date: _____

20 __

---

20 __

---

20 __

---

20 __

---

20 __

Date _____

20 __ 🐞

20 __ ✿

20 __ 🐞

20 __ ✿

20 __ 🐞

Date: _____

20 __ 🐞

_____

_____

_____

_____

20 __ ✿

_____

_____

_____

_____

20 __ 🐞

_____

_____

_____

_____

20 __ ✿

_____

_____

_____

_____

20 __ 🐞

_____

_____

_____

_____

Date _____

20 __ 🐞

20 __ ✿

20 __ 🐞

20 __ ✿

20 __ 🐞

Date: _____

20 __ 🐞

_____
_____
_____
_____

20 __ ✿

_____
_____
_____
_____

20 __ 🐞

_____
_____
_____
_____

20 __ ✿

_____
_____
_____
_____

20 __ 🐞

_____
_____
_____
_____

Date _____

20 __ 🐞
_____
_____
_____
_____

20 __ ✺
_____
_____
_____
_____

20 __ 🐞
_____
_____
_____
_____

20 __ ✺
_____
_____
_____
_____

20 __ 🐞
_____
_____
_____
_____

Date: _____

20 __

_____
_____
_____
_____

20 __

_____
_____
_____
_____

20 __

_____
_____
_____
_____

20 __

_____
_____
_____
_____

20 __

_____
_____
_____
_____

Date _____

20 __ 🐞

_____
_____
_____
_____

20 __ ✿

_____
_____
_____
_____

20 __ 🐞

_____
_____
_____
_____

20 __ ✿

_____
_____
_____
_____

20 __ 🐞

_____
_____
_____
_____

Date: _____

20 __ 🐞

_____
_____
_____
_____

20 __ ❀

_____
_____
_____
_____

20 __ 🐞

_____
_____
_____
_____

20 __ ❀

_____
_____
_____
_____

20 __ 🐞

_____
_____
_____
_____

20 __ 🐞

_____
_____
_____
_____
_____

20 __ ❊

_____
_____
_____
_____

20 __ 🐞

_____
_____
_____
_____

20 __ ❊

_____
_____
_____
_____

20 __ 🐞

_____
_____
_____
_____

Date: _____

20 __ 🐞

20 __ ✿

20 __ 🐞

20 __ ✿

20 __ 🐞

Date _____

20 __ 🐞

_____
_____
_____
_____

20 __ ✿

_____
_____
_____
_____

20 __ 🐞

_____
_____
_____
_____

20 __ ✿

_____
_____
_____
_____

20 __ 🐞

_____
_____
_____
_____

Date: _____

20 __ 🐞

_____
_____
_____
_____
_____

20 __ ❀

_____
_____
_____
_____
_____

20 __ 🐞

_____
_____
_____
_____
_____

20 __ ❀

_____
_____
_____
_____
_____

20 __ 🐞

_____
_____
_____
_____
_____

Date _____

20 __ 🐞

_____
_____
_____
_____

20 __ ✹

_____
_____
_____
_____

20 __ 🐞

_____
_____
_____
_____

20 __ ✻

_____
_____
_____
_____

20 __ 🐞

_____
_____
_____
_____

Date: _____

20 __ 🐞

20 __ ✾

20 __ 🐞

20 __ ✾

20 __ 🐞

Date _____

20 __ 🐞

_____
_____
_____
_____

20 __ ✿

_____
_____
_____
_____

20 __ 🐞

_____
_____
_____
_____

20 __ ✿

_____
_____
_____
_____

20 __ 🐞

_____
_____
_____
_____

Date: _____

20 __ 🐞

20 __ ❀

20 __ 🐞

20 __ ❀

20 __ 🐞

Date _____

20 __ 🐞

_____
_____
_____
_____

20 __ ✿

_____
_____
_____
_____

20 __ 🐞

_____
_____
_____
_____

20 __ ✿

_____
_____
_____
_____

20 __ 🐞

_____
_____
_____
_____

20 __ 🐞

_____
_____
_____
_____

20 __ ✳

_____
_____
_____
_____

20 __ 🐞

_____
_____
_____
_____

20 __ ✳

_____
_____
_____
_____

20 __ 🐞

_____
_____
_____
_____

20 __ 🐞

20 __ ✳

20 __ 🐞

20 __ ✳

20 __ 🐞

Date: _____

20 __ 🐞

20 __ ✾

20 __ 🐞

20 __ ✾

20 __ 🐞

Date _____

20 __ 🐞

20 __ ✸

20 __ 🐞

20 __ ✸

20 __ 🐞

Date: _____

20 __ 🐞

_____
_____
_____
_____

20 __ ❀

_____
_____
_____
_____

20 __ 🐞

_____
_____
_____
_____

20 __ ❀

_____
_____
_____
_____

20 __ 🐞

_____
_____
_____
_____

Date _____

20 __ 🐞

_____
_____
_____
_____

20 __ ❋

_____
_____
_____
_____

20 __ 🐞

_____
_____
_____
_____

20 __ ❋

_____
_____
_____
_____

20 __ 🐞

_____
_____
_____
_____

Date: _____

20 __ 🐞

_____

_____

_____

20 __ ❀

_____

_____

_____

20 __ 🐞

_____

_____

_____

20 __ ❀

_____

_____

_____

20 __ 🐞

_____

_____

_____

Date _____

20 __ 🐞

_____
_____
_____
_____

20 __ ✿

_____
_____
_____
_____

20 __ 🐞

_____
_____
_____
_____

20 __ ✿

_____
_____
_____
_____

20 __ 🐞

_____
_____
_____
_____

Date: _____

20 __ 🐞

_____
_____
_____
_____

20 __ ✳

_____
_____
_____
_____

20 __ 🐞

_____
_____
_____
_____

20 __ ✳

_____
_____
_____
_____

20 __ 🐞

_____
_____
_____
_____

Date _____

20 __ 🐞

_____

_____

_____

20 __ ❄

_____

_____

_____

20 __ 🐞

_____

_____

_____

20 __ ❄

_____

_____

_____

20 __ 🐞

_____

_____

_____

Date: _____

20 __

_____
_____
_____
_____

20 __

_____
_____
_____
_____

20 __

_____
_____
_____
_____

20 __

_____
_____
_____
_____

20 __

_____
_____
_____
_____

Date _____

20 __ 🐞

_____

_____

_____

_____

20 __ ✺

_____

_____

_____

_____

20 __ 🐞

_____

_____

_____

_____

20 __ ✺

_____

_____

_____

_____

20 __ 🐞

_____

_____

_____

_____

Date: _____

20 __ 🐞

_____

_____

_____

_____

_____

20 __ ✳

_____

_____

_____

_____

20 __ 🐞

_____

_____

_____

_____

20 __ ✳

_____

_____

_____

_____

20 __ 🐞

_____

_____

_____

_____

Date _____

20 __

---

20 __

---

20 __

---

20 __

---

20 __

Date: _____

20 __ 🐞

_____
_____
_____
_____

20 __ ❀

_____
_____
_____
_____

20 __ 🐞

_____
_____
_____
_____

20 __ ❀

_____
_____
_____
_____

20 __ 🐞

_____
_____
_____
_____

Date _____

20 __ 🐞

20 __ ✿

20 __ 🐞

20 __ ✿

20 __ 🐞

Date: _____

20 __ 🐞

_____
_____
_____
_____

20 __ ✺

_____
_____
_____
_____

20 __ 🐞

_____
_____
_____
_____

20 __ ✺

_____
_____
_____
_____

20 __ 🐞

_____
_____
_____
_____

Date _____

20 __ 🐞

_____
_____
_____

20 __ ❀

_____
_____
_____

20 __ 🐞

_____
_____
_____

20 __ ❀

_____
_____
_____

20 __ 🐞

_____
_____
_____

Date: _____

20 __ 🐞

_____
_____
_____
_____

20 __ ✿

_____
_____
_____
_____

20 __ 🐞

_____
_____
_____
_____

20 __ ✿

_____
_____
_____
_____

20 __ 🐞

_____
_____
_____
_____

Date _____

20 __ 🐞

_____
_____
_____
_____
_____

20 __ ✿

_____
_____
_____
_____
_____

20 __ 🐞

_____
_____
_____
_____
_____

20 __ ✿

_____
_____
_____
_____
_____

20 __ 🐞

_____
_____
_____
_____
_____

Date: _____

20 __ 🐞

_____
_____
_____
_____
_____

20 __ 🌼

_____
_____
_____
_____
_____

20 __ 🐞

_____
_____
_____
_____
_____

20 __ 🌼

_____
_____
_____
_____
_____

20 __ 🐞

_____
_____
_____
_____
_____

Date _____

20 __ 🐞

_____

_____

_____

_____

20 __ ✿

_____

_____

_____

_____

20 __ 🐞

_____

_____

_____

_____

20 __ ✿

_____

_____

_____

_____

20 __ 🐞

_____

_____

_____

_____

Date: _____

20 __ 🐞

_____
_____
_____
_____
_____

20 __ ✿

_____
_____
_____
_____

20 __ 🐞

_____
_____
_____
_____

20 __ ✿

_____
_____
_____
_____

20 __ 🐞

_____
_____
_____
_____

Date _____

20 __ 🐞

_____
_____
_____
_____

20 __ ❀

_____
_____
_____
_____

20 __ 🐞

_____
_____
_____
_____

20 __ ❀

_____
_____
_____
_____

20 __ 🐞

_____
_____
_____
_____

Date: _____

20 __ 🐞

20 __ ✿

20 __ 🐞

20 __ ✿

20 __ 🐞

Date _____

20 __

_____
_____
_____
_____

20 __

_____
_____
_____
_____

20 __

_____
_____
_____
_____

20 __

_____
_____
_____
_____

20 __

_____
_____
_____
_____

Date: _____

20 __

_____
_____
_____
_____

20 __

_____
_____
_____
_____

20 __

_____
_____
_____
_____

20 __

_____
_____
_____
_____

20 __

_____
_____
_____
_____

Date _____

20 __ 🐞

_____
_____
_____
_____

20 __ ✿

_____
_____
_____
_____

20 __ 🐞

_____
_____
_____
_____

20 __ ✿

_____
_____
_____
_____

20 __ 🐞

_____
_____
_____
_____

Date: _____

20 __

20 __

20 __

20 __

20 __

Date _____

20 __

20 __

20 __

20 __

20 __

Date: _____

20 __

---

20 __

---

20 __

---

20 __

---

20 __

Date _____

20 __ 🐞

20 __ ✳

20 __ 🐞

20 __ ✳

20 __ 🐞

Date: _____

20 __ 🐞

_____

_____

_____

_____

20 __ ✿

_____

_____

_____

_____

20 __ 🐞

_____

_____

_____

_____

20 __ ✿

_____

_____

_____

_____

20 __ 🐞

_____

_____

_____

_____

Date _____

20 __

20 __

20 __

20 __

20 __

Date: _____

20 __

_____
_____
_____
_____

20 __

_____
_____
_____
_____

20 __

_____
_____
_____
_____

20 __

_____
_____
_____
_____

20 __

_____
_____
_____
_____

Date _____

20 __ 🐞

20 __ ✿

20 __ 🐞

20 __ ✿

20 __ 🐞

Date: _____

20 __ 🐞

20 __ ✿

20 __ 🐞

20 __ ✿

20 __ 🐞

Date _____

20 __ 🐞

---

20 __ ✳

---

20 __ 🐞

---

20 __ ✳

---

20 __ 🐞

Date: _____

20 __

20 __

20 __

20 __

20 __

Date _____

20 __ 🐞

_____
_____
_____
_____
_____

20 __ ✿

_____
_____
_____
_____

20 __ 🐞

_____
_____
_____
_____

20 __ ✿

_____
_____
_____
_____

20 __ 🐞

_____
_____
_____
_____

Date: _____

20 __

20 __

20 __

20 __

20 __

20 __ 🐞

20 __ ❀

20 __ 🐞

20 __ ❀

20 __ 🐞

Date: _____

20 __

_____
_____
_____
_____

20 __

_____
_____
_____
_____

20 __

_____
_____
_____
_____

20 __

_____
_____
_____
_____

20 __

_____
_____
_____
_____

20 __ 🐞

_____
_____
_____
_____

20 __ ✿

_____
_____
_____
_____

20 __ 🐞

_____
_____
_____
_____

20 __ ✿

_____
_____
_____
_____

20 __ 🐞

_____
_____
_____
_____

Date: _____

20 __ 🐞

_____

_____

_____

_____

20 __ ❀

_____

_____

_____

_____

20 __ 🐞

_____

_____

_____

_____

20 __ ❀

_____

_____

_____

_____

20 __ 🐞

_____

_____

_____

_____

Date _____

20 __

---

20 __

---

20 __

---

20 __

---

20 __

Date: _____

20 __ 🐞

_____

_____

_____

_____

20 __ ✾

_____

_____

_____

_____

20 __ 🐞

_____

_____

_____

_____

20 __ ✾

_____

_____

_____

_____

20 __ 🐞

_____

_____

_____

_____

Date _____

20 __ 🐞

_____

20 __ ❀

_____

20 __ 🐞

_____

20 __ ❀

_____

20 __ 🐞

_____

Date: _____

20 __

_____

20 __

_____

20 __

_____

20 __

_____

20 __

_____

Date _____

20 __

20 __

20 __

20 __

20 __

Date: _____

20 __ 🐞

_____

_____

_____

_____

20 __ ✿

_____

_____

_____

_____

20 __ 🐞

_____

_____

_____

_____

20 __ ✿

_____

_____

_____

_____

20 __ 🐞

_____

_____

_____

_____

Date _____

20 __ 🐞

20 __ ✽

20 __ 🐞

20 __ ✽

20 __ 🐞

Date: _____

20__ 🐞

_____
_____
_____
_____
_____

20__ ✤

_____
_____
_____
_____
_____

20__ 🐞

_____
_____
_____
_____
_____

20__ ✤

_____
_____
_____
_____
_____

20__ 🐞

_____
_____
_____
_____
_____

Date _____

20 __ 🐞

_____
_____
_____
_____

20 __ ✿

_____
_____
_____
_____

20 __ 🐞

_____
_____
_____
_____

20 __ ✿

_____
_____
_____
_____

20 __ 🐞

_____
_____
_____
_____

Date: _____

20 __ 🐞

_____
_____
_____
_____

20 __ ✺

_____
_____
_____
_____

20 __ 🐞

_____
_____
_____
_____

20 __ ✺

_____
_____
_____
_____

20 __ 🐞

_____
_____
_____
_____

Date _____

20 __ 🐞

_____
_____
_____
_____

20 __ ❀

_____
_____
_____
_____

20 __ 🐞

_____
_____
_____
_____

20 __ ❀

_____
_____
_____
_____

20 __ 🐞

_____
_____
_____
_____

Date: _____

20 __ 🐞

20 __ ❀

20 __ 🐞

20 __ ❀

20 __ 🐞

Date _____

20 __ 🐞

20 __ ❋

20 __ 🐞

20 __ ❋

20 __ 🐞

Date: _____

20 ___ 🐞

_____
_____
_____
_____
_____

20 ___ ✿

_____
_____
_____
_____
_____

20 ___ 🐞

_____
_____
_____
_____
_____

20 ___ ✿

_____
_____
_____
_____
_____

20 ___ 🐞

_____
_____
_____
_____
_____

20 __ 🐞

_____
_____
_____
_____

20 __ ❀

_____
_____
_____
_____

20 __ 🐞

_____
_____
_____
_____

20 __ ❀

_____
_____
_____
_____

20 __ 🐞

_____
_____
_____
_____

Date: _____

20 __ 🐞

_____
_____
_____
_____

20 __ ✽

_____
_____
_____
_____

20 __ 🐞

_____
_____
_____
_____

20 __ ✽

_____
_____
_____
_____

20 __ 🐞

_____
_____
_____
_____

Date _____

20 __ 🐞

_____

_____

_____

_____

20 __ ❋

_____

_____

_____

_____

20 __ 🐞

_____

_____

_____

_____

20 __ ❋

_____

_____

_____

_____

20 __ 🐞

_____

_____

_____

_____

Date: _____

20 __ 🐞

_____
_____
_____
_____

20 __ ✾

_____
_____
_____
_____

20 __ 🐞

_____
_____
_____
_____

20 __ ✾

_____
_____
_____
_____

20 __ 🐞

_____
_____
_____
_____

Date _____

20 __ 🐞

_____
_____
_____
_____

20 __ ✻

_____
_____
_____
_____

20 __ 🐞

_____
_____
_____
_____

20 __ ✻

_____
_____
_____
_____

20 __ 🐞

_____
_____
_____
_____

Date: _____

20 __ 🐞

_____
_____
_____
_____

20 __ ✿

_____
_____
_____
_____

20 __ 🐞

_____
_____
_____
_____

20 __ ✿

_____
_____
_____
_____

20 __ 🐞

_____
_____
_____
_____

Date _____

20 __ 🐞

20 __ ✾

20 __ 🐞

20 __ ✾

20 __ 🐞

Date: _____

20 __ 🐞

_____

_____

_____

_____

20 __ ✿

_____

_____

_____

_____

20 __ 🐞

_____

_____

_____

_____

20 __ ✿

_____

_____

_____

_____

20 __ 🐞

_____

_____

_____

_____

Date _____

20 __ 🐞

_____

_____

_____

_____

20 __ ✻

_____

_____

_____

_____

20 __ 🐞

_____

_____

_____

_____

20 __ ✻

_____

_____

_____

_____

20 __ 🐞

_____

_____

_____

_____

Date: _____

20 __ 🐞

20 __ ✿

20 __ 🐞

20 __ ✿

20 __ 🐞

Date _____

20 __ 🐞
_____
_____
_____
_____

20 __ ✿
_____
_____
_____
_____

20 __ 🐞
_____
_____
_____
_____

20 __ ✿
_____
_____
_____
_____

20 __ 🐞
_____
_____
_____
_____

20 __ 🐞

_____

_____

_____

_____

20 __ ✳

_____

_____

_____

_____

20 __ 🐞

_____

_____

_____

_____

20 __ ✳

_____

_____

_____

_____

20 __ 🐞

_____

_____

_____

_____

Date _____

20 __ 🐞

_____
_____
_____
_____

20 __ ❀

_____
_____
_____
_____

20 __ 🐞

_____
_____
_____
_____

20 __ ❀

_____
_____
_____
_____

20 __ 🐞

_____
_____
_____
_____

Date: _____

20 __ 🐞

20 __ ✾

20 __ 🐞

20 __ ✾

20 __ 🐞

Date _____

20 __

20 __

20 __

20 __

20 __

Date: _____

20 __ 🐞

_____

_____

_____

20 __ ✿

_____

_____

_____

20 __ 🐞

_____

_____

_____

20 __ ✿

_____

_____

_____

20 __ 🐞

_____

_____

_____

Date _____

20 __

_____
_____
_____
_____

20 __

_____
_____
_____
_____

20 __

_____
_____
_____
_____

20 __

_____
_____
_____
_____

20 __

_____
_____
_____
_____

Date: _____

20 __ 🐞

_____
_____
_____
_____

20 __ ❋

_____
_____
_____
_____

20 __ 🐞

_____
_____
_____
_____

20 __ ❋

_____
_____
_____
_____

20 __ 🐞

_____
_____
_____
_____

Date _____

20 __ 🐞

_____
_____
_____
_____

20 __ ❁

_____
_____
_____
_____

20 __ 🐞

_____
_____
_____
_____

20 __ ❁

_____
_____
_____
_____

20 __ 🐞

_____
_____
_____
_____

Date: _____

20 __

20 __

20 __

20 __

20 __

Date _____

20 __ 🐞

_____

_____

_____

_____

20 __ ✳

_____

_____

_____

_____

20 __ 🐞

_____

_____

_____

_____

20 __ ✳

_____

_____

_____

_____

20 __ 🐞

_____

_____

_____

_____

Date: _____

20 __ 🐞

20 __ ✿

20 __ 🐞

20 __ ✿

20 __ 🐞

Date _____

20 __ 🐞

_____
_____
_____
_____

20 __ ❀

_____
_____
_____
_____

20 __ 🐞

_____
_____
_____
_____

20 __ ❀

_____
_____
_____
_____

20 __ 🐞

_____
_____
_____
_____

20 __

20 __

20 __

20 __

20 __

Date _____

20 __ 🐞

_____
_____
_____
_____

20 __ ✻

_____
_____
_____
_____

20 __ 🐞

_____
_____
_____
_____

20 __ ✻

_____
_____
_____
_____

20 __ 🐞

_____
_____
_____
_____

Date: _____

20 __

---

20 __

---

20 __

---

20 __

---

20 __

Date _____

20 __ 🐞

_____
_____
_____
_____

20 __ ✿

_____
_____
_____
_____

20 __ 🐞

_____
_____
_____
_____

20 __ ✿

_____
_____
_____
_____

20 __ 🐞

_____
_____
_____
_____

Date: _____

20 __ 🐞

_____
_____
_____
_____

20 __ ❀

_____
_____
_____
_____

20 __ 🐞

_____
_____
_____
_____

20 __ ❀

_____
_____
_____
_____

20 __ 🐞

_____
_____
_____
_____

Date _____

20 __ 🐞

_____
_____
_____
_____

20 __ ❀

_____
_____
_____
_____

20 __ 🐞

_____
_____
_____
_____

20 __ ❀

_____
_____
_____
_____

20 __ 🐞

_____
_____
_____
_____

Date: _____

20 __ 🐞

20 __ ❀

20 __ 🐞

20 __ ❀

20 __ 🐞

Date _____

20 __

---

20 __

---

20 __

---

20 __

---

20 __

Date: _____

20 __ 🐞

_____
_____
_____
_____

20 __ ✿

_____
_____
_____
_____

20 __ 🐞

_____
_____
_____
_____

20 __ ✿

_____
_____
_____
_____

20 __ 🐞

_____
_____
_____
_____

Date _____

20 __ 🐞

_____
_____
_____
_____

20 __ ✿

_____
_____
_____
_____

20 __ 🐞

_____
_____
_____
_____

20 __ ✿

_____
_____
_____
_____

20 __ 🐞

_____
_____
_____
_____

Date: _____

20 __

20 __

20 __

20 __

20 __

Date _____

20 __ 🐞

_____

20 __ ❁

_____

20 __ 🐞

_____

20 __ ❁

_____

20 __ 🐞

_____

Date: _____

20 __ 🐞

_____

_____

_____

_____

20 __ ✺

_____

_____

_____

_____

20 __ 🐞

_____

_____

_____

_____

20 __ ✺

_____

_____

_____

_____

20 __ 🐞

_____

_____

_____

_____

Date _____

20 __ 🐞

20 __ ✾

20 __ 🐞

20 __ ✾

20 __ 🐞

Date: _____

20 __ 🐞

_____
_____
_____
_____

20 __ ✿

_____
_____
_____
_____

20 __ 🐞

_____
_____
_____
_____

20 __ ✿

_____
_____
_____
_____

20 __ 🐞

_____
_____
_____
_____

Date _____

20 __ 🐞

_____
_____
_____
_____
_____

20 __ ✳

_____
_____
_____
_____
_____

20 __ 🐞

_____
_____
_____
_____
_____

20 __ ✳

_____
_____
_____
_____
_____

20 __ 🐞

_____
_____
_____
_____
_____

Date: _____

20 __ 🐞

20 __ ✿

20 __ 🐞

20 __ ✿

20 __ 🐞

Date _____

20 __

---

20 __

---

20 __

---

20 __

---

20 __

Date: _____

20 __

20 __

20 __

20 __

20 __

Date _____

20 __ 🐞

_____
_____
_____
_____

20 __ ✿

_____
_____
_____
_____

20 __ 🐞

_____
_____
_____
_____

20 __ ✿

_____
_____
_____
_____

20 __ 🐞

_____
_____
_____
_____

Date: _____

20 __

20 __

20 __

20 __

20 __

Date _____

20 __ 🐞

_____
_____
_____
_____

20 __ ✿

_____
_____
_____
_____

20 __ 🐞

_____
_____
_____
_____

20 __ ✿

_____
_____
_____
_____

20 __ 🐞

_____
_____
_____
_____

Date: _____

20 __ 🐞

_____

_____

_____

_____

20 __ ❁

_____

_____

_____

_____

20 __ 🐞

_____

_____

_____

_____

20 __ ❁

_____

_____

_____

_____

20 __ 🐞

_____

_____

_____

_____

Date _____

20 __ 🐞

_____

_____

_____

_____

20 __ ✿

_____

_____

_____

_____

20 __ 🐞

_____

_____

_____

_____

20 __ ✿

_____

_____

_____

_____

20 __ 🐞

_____

_____

_____

_____

Date: _____

20 __

20 __

20 __

20 __

20 __

Date _____

20 __ 🐞

_____

20 __ ✿

_____

20 __ 🐞

_____

20 __ ✿

_____

20 __ 🐞

Date: _____

20 __

---

20 __

---

20 __

---

20 __

---

20 __

Date _____

20 __ 🐞

_____
_____
_____
_____
_____

20 __ ❀

_____
_____
_____
_____
_____

20 __ 🐞

_____
_____
_____
_____
_____

20 __ ❀

_____
_____
_____
_____
_____

20 __ 🐞

_____
_____
_____
_____
_____

20 __

---

20 __

---

20 __

---

20 __

---

20 __

Date _____

20 __ 🐞

_____
_____
_____
_____

20 __ ❀

_____
_____
_____
_____

20 __ 🐞

_____
_____
_____
_____

20 __ ❀

_____
_____
_____
_____

20 __ 🐞

_____
_____
_____
_____

Date: _____

20 __ 🐞

20 __ ✿

20 __ 🐞

20 __ ✿

20 __ 🐞

Date _____

20 __ 🐞

_____
_____
_____
_____
_____

20 __ ❀

_____
_____
_____
_____
_____

20 __ 🐞

_____
_____
_____
_____
_____

20 __ ❀

_____
_____
_____
_____
_____

20 __ 🐞

_____
_____
_____
_____
_____

Date: _____

20 __ 🐞

_____
_____
_____
_____

20 __ ✿

_____
_____
_____
_____

20 __ 🐞

_____
_____
_____
_____

20 __ ✿

_____
_____
_____
_____

20 __ 🐞

_____
_____
_____
_____

Date _____

20 ___ 🐞

_____
_____
_____
_____

20 ___ ❀

_____
_____
_____
_____

20 ___ 🐞

_____
_____
_____
_____

20 ___ ❀

_____
_____
_____
_____

20 ___ 🐞

_____
_____
_____
_____

Date: _____

20 __ 🐞

_____
_____
_____
_____

20 __ ❁

_____
_____
_____

20 __ 🐞

_____
_____
_____

20 __ ❁

_____
_____
_____

20 __ 🐞

_____
_____
_____

Date _____

20 __

20 __

20 __

20 __

20 __

Date: _____

20 __

20 __

20 __

20 __

20 __

Date _____

20 __

_____

_____

_____

_____

20 __

_____

_____

_____

_____

20 __

_____

_____

_____

_____

20 __

_____

_____

_____

_____

20 __

_____

_____

_____

_____

Date: _____

20 __

---

20 __

---

20 __

---

20 __

---

20 __

Date _____

20 __ 🐞

_____
_____
_____
_____

20 __ ✿

_____
_____
_____

20 __ 🐞

_____
_____
_____
_____

20 __ ✿

_____
_____
_____
_____

20 __ 🐞

_____
_____
_____
_____

Date: _____

20 __ 🐞

_____

_____

_____

_____

20 __ ✤

_____

_____

_____

_____

20 __ 🐞

_____

_____

_____

_____

20 __ ✤

_____

_____

_____

_____

20 __ 🐞

_____

_____

_____

_____

Date _____

20 __ 🐞

_____

_____

_____

_____

20 __ ✿

_____

_____

_____

_____

20 __ 🐞

_____

_____

_____

_____

20 __ ✿

_____

_____

_____

_____

20 __ 🐞

_____

_____

_____

_____

Date: _____

20 __

20 __

20 __

20 __

20 __

Date _____

20 __ 🐞

20 __ ✿

20 __ 🐞

20 __ ✿

20 __ 🐞

Date: _____

20 __ 🐞

_____

_____

_____

_____

20 __ ✿

_____

_____

_____

_____

20 __ 🐞

_____

_____

_____

_____

20 __ ✿

_____

_____

_____

_____

20 __ 🐞

_____

_____

_____

_____

Date _____

20 __

20 __

20 __

20 __

20 __

Date: _____

20 __

_____

_____

_____

20 __

_____

_____

_____

20 __

_____

_____

_____

20 __

_____

_____

_____

20 __

_____

_____

Date _____

20 __ 🐞

_____
_____
_____
_____

20 __ ✳

_____
_____
_____
_____

20 __ 🐞

_____
_____
_____
_____

20 __ ✳

_____
_____
_____
_____

20 __ 🐞

_____
_____
_____
_____

Date: _____

20 __ 🐞

_____

_____

_____

20 __ ✿

_____

_____

_____

20 __ 🐞

_____

_____

_____

20 __ ✿

_____

_____

_____

20 __ 🐞

_____

_____

_____

Date _____

20 __

---

20 __

---

20 __

---

20 __

---

20 __

Date: _____

20 __ 🐞

_____

_____

_____

_____

20 __ ✿

_____

_____

_____

_____

20 __ 🐞

_____

_____

_____

_____

20 __ ✿

_____

_____

_____

_____

20 __ 🐞

_____

_____

_____

_____

Date _____

20 __ 🐞

_____
_____
_____
_____
_____

20 __ ✿

_____
_____
_____
_____
_____

20 __ 🐞

_____
_____
_____
_____
_____

20 __ ✿

_____
_____
_____
_____
_____

20 __ 🐞

_____
_____
_____
_____
_____

Date: _____

20 __ 🐞

_____

_____

_____

_____

20 __ ✿

_____

_____

_____

_____

20 __ 🐞

_____

_____

_____

_____

20 __ ✿

_____

_____

_____

_____

20 __ 🐞

_____

_____

_____

_____

Date _____

20 __ 🐞

_____

_____

_____

_____

20 __ ❀

_____

_____

_____

_____

20 __ 🐞

_____

_____

_____

_____

20 __ ❀

_____

_____

_____

_____

20 __ 🐞

_____

_____

_____

_____

Date: _____

20 __

20 __

20 __

20 __

20 __

Date _____

20 __ 🐞

_____
_____
_____
_____

20 __ ❀

_____
_____
_____
_____

20 __ 🐞

_____
_____
_____
_____

20 __ ❀

_____
_____
_____
_____

20 __ 🐞

_____
_____
_____
_____

Date: _____

20 __

_____
_____
_____
_____

20 __

_____
_____
_____
_____

20 __

_____
_____
_____
_____

20 __

_____
_____
_____
_____

20 __

_____
_____
_____
_____

Date _____

20 __

_____

_____

_____

20 __

_____

_____

_____

20 __

_____

_____

_____

20 __

_____

_____

_____

20 __

_____

_____

_____

Date: _____

20 __ 🐞

_____

20 __ ❀

_____

20 __ 🐞

_____

20 __ ❀

_____

20 __ 🐞

_____

Date _____

20 __

_____
_____
_____
_____

20 __

_____
_____
_____
_____

20 __

_____
_____
_____
_____

20 __

_____
_____
_____
_____

20 __

_____
_____
_____
_____

Date: _____

20 __ 🐞

_____

20 __ ✳

_____

20 __ 🐞

_____

20 __ ✳

_____

20 __ 🐞

_____

Date _____

20 __

_____
_____
_____
_____
_____

20 __

_____
_____
_____
_____

20 __

_____
_____
_____
_____

20 __

_____
_____
_____
_____

20 __

_____
_____
_____
_____

Date: _____

20 __ 🐞

_____

_____

_____

_____

20 __ ❀

_____

_____

_____

_____

20 __ 🐞

_____

_____

_____

_____

20 __ ❀

_____

_____

_____

_____

20 __ 🐞

_____

_____

_____

_____

Date _____

20 __ 🐞

_____
_____
_____
_____
_____

20 __ ✿

_____
_____
_____
_____
_____

20 __ 🐞

_____
_____
_____
_____
_____

20 __ ✿

_____
_____
_____
_____
_____

20 __ 🐞

_____
_____
_____
_____
_____

Date: _____

20 __

---

20 __

---

20 __

---

20 __

---

20 __

Date _____

20 __ 🐞

_____
_____
_____
_____

20 __ ❀

_____
_____
_____
_____

20 __ 🐞

_____
_____
_____
_____

20 __ ❀

_____
_____
_____
_____

20 __ 🐞

_____
_____
_____
_____

Date: _____

20 __ 🐞

_____

_____

_____

_____

20 __ ✺

_____

_____

_____

_____

20 __ 🐞

_____

_____

_____

_____

20 __ ✾

_____

_____

_____

_____

20 __ 🐞

_____

_____

_____

_____

Date _____

20 __

---

20 __

---

20 __

---

20 __

---

20 __

Date: _____

20 __ 🐞

_____
_____
_____
_____

20 __ ✲

_____
_____
_____
_____

20 __ 🐞

_____
_____
_____
_____

20 __ ✲

_____
_____
_____
_____

20 __ 🐞

_____
_____
_____
_____

Date _____

20 __ 🐞

_____

_____

_____

_____

20 __ ✿

_____

_____

_____

_____

20 __ 🐞

_____

_____

_____

_____

20 __ ✿

_____

_____

_____

_____

20 __ 🐞

_____

_____

_____

_____

Date: _____

20 __ 🐞

_____
_____
_____
_____

20 __ ✿

_____
_____
_____
_____

20 __ 🐞

_____
_____
_____
_____

20 __ ✿

_____
_____
_____
_____

20 __ 🐞

_____
_____
_____
_____

Date _____

20 __ 🐞

_____

20 __ ✿

_____

20 __ 🐞

_____

20 __ ✿

_____

20 __ 🐞

_____

Date: _____

20 __

_____
_____
_____
_____

20 __

_____
_____
_____
_____

20 __

_____
_____
_____
_____

20 __

_____
_____
_____
_____

20 __

_____
_____
_____
_____

Date _____

20 __ 🐞

_____
_____
_____
_____

20 __ ✳

_____
_____
_____
_____

20 __ 🐞

_____
_____
_____
_____

20 __ ✳

_____
_____
_____
_____

20 __ 🐞

_____
_____
_____
_____

Date: _____

20 __

20 __

20 __

20 __

20 __

Date _____

20 __

_____
_____
_____
_____
_____

20 __

_____
_____
_____
_____
_____

20 __

_____
_____
_____
_____
_____

20 __

_____
_____
_____
_____
_____

20 __

_____
_____
_____
_____
_____

Date: _____

20 __

20 __

20 __

20 __

20 __

Date _____

20 __ 🐞

_____
_____
_____
_____

20 __ ❀

_____
_____
_____
_____

20 __ 🐞

_____
_____
_____
_____

20 __ ❀

_____
_____
_____
_____

20 __ 🐞

_____
_____
_____
_____

Date: _____

20 __ 🐞

_____
_____
_____
_____

20 __ ✿

_____
_____
_____
_____

20 __ 🐞

_____
_____
_____
_____

20 __ ✿

_____
_____
_____
_____

20 __ 🐞

_____
_____
_____
_____

Date _____

20 __

---

20 __

---

20 __

---

20 __

---

20 __

Date: _____

20 __

20 __

20 __

20 __

20 __

Date _____

20 __ 🐞

20 __ ✿

20 __ 🐞

20 __ ✿

20 __ 🐞

Date: _____

20 __ 🐞

_____

_____

_____

20 __ ✿

_____

_____

_____

20 __ 🐞

_____

_____

_____

20 __ ✿

_____

_____

_____

20 __ 🐞

_____

_____

_____

Date _____

20 __ 🐞

_____
_____
_____
_____

20 __ ✿

_____
_____
_____
_____

20 __ 🐞

_____
_____
_____
_____

20 __ ✿

_____
_____
_____
_____

20 __ 🐞

_____
_____
_____
_____

Date: _____

20 __ 🐞

_____
_____
_____
_____

20 __ ❀

_____
_____
_____
_____

20 __ 🐞

_____
_____
_____
_____

20 __ ❀

_____
_____
_____
_____

20 __ 🐞

_____
_____
_____
_____

Date _____

20 __

20 __

20 __

20 __

20 __

Date: _____

20 __

_____

_____

_____

20 __

_____

_____

_____

20 __

_____

_____

_____

20 __

_____

_____

_____

20 __

_____

_____

_____

Date _____

20 __ 🐞

_____
_____
_____
_____

20 __ ✿

_____
_____
_____
_____

20 __ 🐞

_____
_____
_____
_____

20 __ ✿

_____
_____
_____
_____

20 __ 🐞

_____
_____
_____
_____

Date: _____

20 __

_____
_____
_____
_____

20 __

_____
_____
_____
_____

20 __

_____
_____
_____
_____

20 __

_____
_____
_____
_____

20 __

_____
_____
_____

Date _____

20 __ 🐞

_____
_____
_____
_____

20 __ ✺

_____
_____
_____
_____

20 __ 🐞

_____
_____
_____
_____

20 __ ✺

_____
_____
_____
_____

20 __ 🐞

_____
_____
_____
_____

Date: _____

20 __ 🐞

_____

_____

_____

20 __ ✿

_____

_____

_____

20 __ 🐞

_____

_____

_____

20 __ ✿

_____

_____

_____

20 __ 🐞

_____

_____

_____

Date _____

20 __

20 __

20 __

20 __

20 __

Date: _____

20 __ 🐞

_____

_____

_____

20 __ ✿

_____

_____

_____

20 __ 🐞

_____

_____

_____

20 __ ✿

_____

_____

_____

20 __ 🐞

_____

_____

_____

Date _____

20 __ 🐞
_____
_____
_____
_____

20 __ 🌼
_____
_____
_____
_____

20 __ 🐞
_____
_____
_____
_____

20 __ 🌼
_____
_____
_____
_____

20 __ 🐞
_____
_____
_____
_____

Date: _____

20 __ 🐞

_____
_____
_____
_____

20 __ ✿

_____
_____
_____
_____

20 __ 🐞

_____
_____
_____
_____

20 __ ✿

_____
_____
_____
_____

20 __ 🐞

_____
_____
_____
_____

Date _____

20 __ 🐞

_____

_____

_____

_____

20 __ �֍

_____

_____

_____

_____

20 __ 🐞

_____

_____

_____

_____

20 __ �֍

_____

_____

_____

_____

20 __ 🐞

_____

_____

_____

_____

Date: _____

20 __

20 __

20 __

20 __

20 __

Date _____

20 __ 🐞

20 __ ✿

20 __ 🐞

20 __ ✿

20 __ 🐞

Date: _____

20 __ 🐞

_____
_____
_____
_____

20 __ ✺

_____
_____
_____
_____

20 __ 🐞

_____
_____
_____
_____

20 __ ✺

_____
_____
_____
_____

20 __ 🐞

_____
_____
_____
_____

Date _____

20 __ 🐞

_____
_____
_____
_____

20 __ ✿

_____
_____
_____
_____

20 __ 🐞

_____
_____
_____
_____

20 __ ✿

_____
_____
_____
_____

20 __ 🐞

_____
_____
_____
_____

Date: _____

20 __ 🐞

_____

_____

_____

20 __ ❀

_____

_____

_____

20 __ 🐞

_____

_____

_____

20 __ ❀

_____

_____

_____

20 __ 🐞

_____

_____

_____

Date _____

20 __ 🐞

_____
_____
_____
_____

20 __ ✿

_____
_____
_____
_____

20 __ 🐞

_____
_____
_____
_____

20 __ ✿

_____
_____
_____
_____

20 __ 🐞

_____
_____
_____

Date: _____

20 __ 🐞

_____

_____

_____

_____

20 __ ✿

_____

_____

_____

_____

20 __ 🐞

_____

_____

_____

_____

20 __ ✿

_____

_____

_____

_____

20 __ 🐞

_____

_____

_____

_____

Date _____

20 __

_____
_____
_____
_____

20 __

_____
_____
_____
_____

20 __

_____
_____
_____
_____

20 __

_____
_____
_____
_____

20 __

_____
_____
_____
_____

Date: _____

20 __ 🐞

_____
_____
_____
_____

20 __ ✳

_____
_____
_____

20 __ 🐞

_____
_____
_____

20 __ ✳

_____
_____
_____

20 __ 🐞

_____
_____
_____

Date _____

20 __ 🐞
_____
_____
_____
_____

20 __ ✿
_____
_____
_____
_____

20 __ 🐞
_____
_____
_____
_____

20 __ ✿
_____
_____
_____
_____

20 __ 🐞
_____
_____
_____
_____

Date: _____

20 __

20 __

20 __

20 __

20 __

Date _____

20 __ 🐞

_____
_____
_____
_____
_____

20 __ ✳

_____
_____
_____
_____
_____

20 __ 🐞

_____
_____
_____
_____
_____

20 __ ✳

_____
_____
_____
_____
_____

20 __ 🐞

_____
_____
_____
_____
_____

Date: _____

20 __

20 __

20 __

20 __

20 __

Date _____

20 __ 🐞

_____

_____

_____

_____

20 __ ✿

_____

_____

_____

_____

20 __ 🐞

_____

_____

_____

_____

20 __ ✿

_____

_____

_____

_____

20 __ 🐞

_____

_____

_____

_____

Date: _____

20 __ 🐞

_____

_____

_____

_____

20 __ 🌼

_____

_____

_____

_____

20 __ 🐞

_____

_____

_____

_____

20 __ 🌼

_____

_____

_____

_____

20 __ 🐞

_____

_____

_____

_____

Date _____

20 __ 🐞

_____
_____
_____
_____
_____

20 __ ✿

_____
_____
_____
_____
_____

20 __ 🐞

_____
_____
_____
_____
_____

20 __ ✿

_____
_____
_____
_____
_____

20 __ 🐞

_____
_____
_____
_____

Date: _____

20 __ 🐞

_____
_____
_____
_____

20 __ ✺

_____
_____
_____
_____

20 __ 🐞

_____
_____
_____
_____

20 __ ✺

_____
_____
_____
_____

20 __ 🐞

_____
_____
_____
_____

Date _____

20 __ 🐞

_____
_____
_____
_____

20 __ ✾

_____
_____
_____
_____

20 __ 🐞

_____
_____
_____
_____

20 __ ✾

_____
_____
_____
_____

20 __ 🐞

_____
_____
_____
_____

Date: _____

20 __

_____
_____
_____
_____

20 __

_____
_____
_____
_____

20 __

_____
_____
_____
_____

20 __

_____
_____
_____
_____

20 __

_____
_____
_____
_____

Date _____

20 __ 🐞

_____

_____

_____

_____

20 __ ✳

_____

_____

_____

_____

20 __ 🐞

_____

_____

_____

_____

20 __ ✳

_____

_____

_____

_____

20 __ 🐞

_____

_____

_____

_____

Date: _____

20 __

_____

_____

_____

20 __

_____

_____

_____

20 __

_____

_____

_____

20 __

_____

_____

_____

20 __

_____

_____

_____

Date _____

20 __ 🐞

20 __ ❀

20 __ 🐞

20 __ ❀

20 __ 🐞

Date: _____

20 __ 🐞
_____
_____
_____

20 __ ❁
_____
_____
_____

20 __ 🐞
_____
_____
_____

20 __ ❁
_____
_____
_____

20 __ 🐞
_____
_____

Date _____

20 __ 🐞
_____
_____
_____
_____

20 __ ✾
_____
_____
_____
_____

20 __ 🐞
_____
_____
_____
_____

20 __ ✾
_____
_____
_____
_____

20 __ 🐞
_____
_____
_____
_____

20 __

_____
_____
_____
_____

20 __

_____
_____
_____
_____

20 __

_____
_____
_____
_____

20 __

_____
_____
_____
_____

20 __

_____
_____
_____

Date _____

20 __ 🐞

_____
_____
_____
_____

20 __ ✿

_____
_____
_____
_____

20 __ 🐞

_____
_____
_____
_____

20 __ ✿

_____
_____
_____
_____

20 __ 🐞

_____
_____
_____
_____

Date: _____

20 __

_____
_____
_____
_____

20 __

_____
_____
_____
_____

20 __

_____
_____
_____
_____

20 __

_____
_____
_____
_____

20 __

_____
_____
_____

Date _____

20 __ 🐞

_____
_____
_____
_____

20 __ ✿

_____
_____
_____
_____

20 __ 🐞

_____
_____
_____
_____

20 __ ✿

_____
_____
_____
_____

20 __ 🐞

_____
_____
_____
_____

Date: _____

20 __

20 __

20 __

20 __

20 __

Date _____

20 __ 🐞

_____
_____
_____
_____

20 __ ✿

_____
_____
_____
_____

20 __ 🐞

_____
_____
_____
_____

20 __ ✿

_____
_____
_____
_____

20 __ 🐞

_____
_____
_____
_____

Date: _____

20 __ 🐞

_____
_____
_____
_____

20 __ ✳

_____
_____
_____
_____

20 __ 🐞

_____
_____
_____
_____

20 __ ✳

_____
_____
_____
_____

20 __ 🐞

_____
_____
_____

Date _____

20 __ 🐞

_____

_____

_____

20 __ ✿

_____

_____

_____

20 __ 🐞

_____

_____

_____

20 __ ✿

_____

_____

_____

20 __ 🐞

_____

_____

_____

Date: _____

20 __

_____
_____
_____
_____

20 __

_____
_____
_____
_____

20 __

_____
_____
_____
_____

20 __

_____
_____
_____
_____

20 __

_____
_____
_____

Date _____

20 ___ 🐞

_____
_____
_____
_____

20 ___ ❀

_____
_____
_____
_____

20 ___ 🐞

_____
_____
_____
_____

20 ___ ❀

_____
_____
_____
_____

20 ___ 🐞

_____
_____
_____
_____

Date: _____

20 __ 🐞

_____
_____
_____
_____

20 __ ✺

_____
_____
_____
_____

20 __ 🐞

_____
_____
_____
_____

20 __ ✺

_____
_____
_____
_____

20 __ 🐞

_____
_____
_____

Date _____

20 __ 🐞

_____

_____

_____

20 __ ❀

_____

_____

_____

20 __ 🐞

_____

_____

_____

20 __ ❀

_____

_____

_____

20 __ 🐞

_____

_____

_____

Date: _____

20 __

20 __

20 __

20 __

20 __

Date _____

20 __ 🐞

_____

20 __ ✿

_____

20 __ 🐞

_____

20 __ ✿

_____

20 __ 🐞

_____

Date: _____

20 __ 🐞

_____

_____

_____

20 __ ✾

_____

_____

_____

20 __ 🐞

_____

_____

_____

20 __ ✾

_____

_____

_____

20 __ 🐞

_____

_____

_____

Date _____

20 __ 🐞

_____
_____
_____
_____

20 __ ❀

_____
_____
_____
_____

20 __ 🐞

_____
_____
_____
_____

20 __ ❀

_____
_____
_____
_____

20 __ 🐞

_____
_____
_____
_____

Date: _____

20 __

_____
_____
_____
_____

20 __

_____
_____
_____
_____

20 __

_____
_____
_____
_____

20 __

_____
_____
_____
_____

20 __

_____
_____
_____

Date _____

20 __ 🐞

_____
_____
_____
_____

20 __ ✳

_____
_____
_____
_____

20 __ 🐞

_____
_____
_____
_____

20 __ ✳

_____
_____
_____
_____

20 __ 🐞

_____
_____
_____
_____

Date: _____

20 __ 🐞

_____

20 __ ✿

_____

20 __ 🐞

_____

20 __ ✿

_____

20 __ 🐞

_____

Date _____

20 __ 🐞

_____

20 __ ❀

_____

20 __ 🐞

_____

20 __ ❀

_____

20 __ 🐞

_____

Date: _____

20 __

---

20 __

---

20 __

---

20 __

---

20 __

Date _____

20 __ 🐞

_____

_____

_____

20 __ ✳

_____

_____

_____

20 __ 🐞

_____

_____

_____

20 __ ✳

_____

_____

_____

20 __ 🐞

_____

_____

_____

Date: _____

20 __

_____

_____

_____

_____

20 __

_____

_____

_____

_____

20 __

_____

_____

_____

_____

20 __

_____

_____

_____

_____

20 __

_____

_____

_____

_____

Date _____

20 __ 🐞

_____
_____
_____
_____

20 __ ❀

_____
_____
_____
_____

20 __ 🐞

_____
_____
_____
_____

20 __ ❀

_____
_____
_____
_____

20 __ 🐞

_____
_____
_____
_____

Date: _____

20 __ 🐞

20 __ ✳

20 __ 🐞

20 __ ✳

20 __ 🐞

Date _____

20 __ 🐞

_____
_____
_____
_____

20 __ ✻

_____
_____
_____
_____

20 __ 🐞

_____
_____
_____
_____

20 __ ✿

_____
_____
_____
_____

20 __ 🐞

_____
_____
_____
_____

Date: _____

20 __

20 __

20 __

20 __

20 __

Date _____

20 __

_____
_____
_____
_____

20 __

_____
_____
_____
_____

20 __

_____
_____
_____
_____

20 __

_____
_____
_____
_____

20 __

_____
_____
_____
_____

Date: _____

20 __ 🐞

_____
_____
_____
_____

20 __ ✳

_____
_____
_____
_____

20 __ 🐞

_____
_____
_____
_____

20 __ ✳

_____
_____
_____
_____

20 __ 🐞

_____
_____
_____
_____

Date _____

20 __

---

20 __

---

20 __

---

20 __

---

20 __

Date: _____

20 __ 🐞

_____

_____

_____

_____

20 __ ✿

_____

_____

_____

_____

20 __ 🐞

_____

_____

_____

_____

20 __ ✿

_____

_____

_____

_____

20 __ 🐞

_____

_____

_____

_____

Date _____

20 __ 🐞

_____
_____
_____
_____

20 __ ✿

_____
_____
_____
_____

20 __ 🐞

_____
_____
_____
_____

20 __ ✿

_____
_____
_____
_____

20 __ 🐞

_____
_____
_____
_____

Date: _____

20 __ 🐞

_____

_____

_____

20 __ ❀

_____

_____

_____

20 __ 🐞

_____

_____

_____

20 __ ❀

_____

_____

_____

20 __ 🐞

_____

_____

_____

Date _____

20 __ 🐞

_____
_____
_____
_____

20 __ ✼

_____
_____
_____
_____

20 __ 🐞

_____
_____
_____
_____

20 __ ✼

_____
_____
_____
_____

20 __ 🐞

_____
_____
_____
_____

Date: _____

20 __ 🐞

20 __ ✾

20 __ 🐞

20 __ ✾

20 __ 🐞

Date _____

20 __ 🐞

_____
_____
_____
_____

20 __ ❀

_____
_____
_____
_____

20 __ 🐞

_____
_____
_____
_____

20 __ ❀

_____
_____
_____
_____

20 __ 🐞

_____
_____
_____

Date: _____

20 __ 🐞

20 __ ✿

20 __ 🐞

20 __ ✿

20 __ 🐞

Date _____

20 __ 🐞

_____
_____
_____
_____

20 __ ❀

_____
_____
_____
_____

20 __ 🐞

_____
_____
_____
_____

20 __ ❀

_____
_____
_____
_____

20 __ 🐞

_____
_____
_____
_____

Date: _____

20 __

---

20 __

---

20 __

---

20 __

---

20 __

Date _____

20 __ 🐞

_____
_____
_____
_____

20 __ ✿

_____
_____
_____
_____

20 __ 🐞

_____
_____
_____
_____

20 __ ✿

_____
_____
_____
_____

20 __ 🐞

_____
_____
_____
_____

Date: _____

20 __

20 __

20 __

20 __

20 __

Date _____

20 __ 🐞

_____
_____
_____
_____

20 __ ✿

_____
_____
_____
_____

20 __ 🐞

_____
_____
_____
_____

20 __ ✿

_____
_____
_____
_____

20 __ 🐞

_____
_____
_____
_____

Date: _____

20 __

20 __

20 __

20 __

20 __

Date _____

20 __ 🐞

_____
_____
_____
_____

20 __ ✿

_____
_____
_____
_____

20 __ 🐞

_____
_____
_____
_____

20 __ ✿

_____
_____
_____
_____

20 __ 🐞

_____
_____
_____
_____

Date: _____

20 __ 🐞

_____
_____
_____
_____

20 __ ✾

_____
_____
_____
_____

20 __ 🐞

_____
_____
_____
_____

20 __ ✾

_____
_____
_____
_____

20 __ 🐞

_____
_____
_____
_____

20 __ 🐞

_____

_____

_____

_____

20 __ ❁

_____

_____

_____

_____

20 __ 🐞

_____

_____

_____

_____

20 __ ❁

_____

_____

_____

_____

20 __ 🐞

_____

_____

_____

_____

Date: _____

20 __ 🐞

20 __ ✿

20 __ 🐞

20 __ ✿

20 __ 🐞

Date _____

20 __ 🐞

20 __ ✿

20 __ 🐞

20 __ ✿

20 __ 🐞

Date: _____

20 __ 🐞

_____

_____

_____

20 __ ✺

_____

_____

_____

20 __ 🐞

_____

_____

_____

20 __ ✺

_____

_____

_____

20 __ 🐞

_____

_____

_____

Date _____

20 __

_____
_____
_____
_____

20 __

_____
_____
_____
_____

20 __

_____
_____
_____
_____

20 __

_____
_____
_____
_____

20 __

_____
_____
_____
_____

Date: _____

20 __ 🐞

_____
_____
_____
_____

20 __ ❀

_____
_____
_____
_____

20 __ 🐞

_____
_____
_____
_____

20 __ ❀

_____
_____
_____
_____

20 __ 🐞

_____
_____
_____
_____

Made in the USA
Columbia, SC
22 June 2023

18554123R00202